HONEY FARMS

FUNKY FARMS

Lynn M. Stone

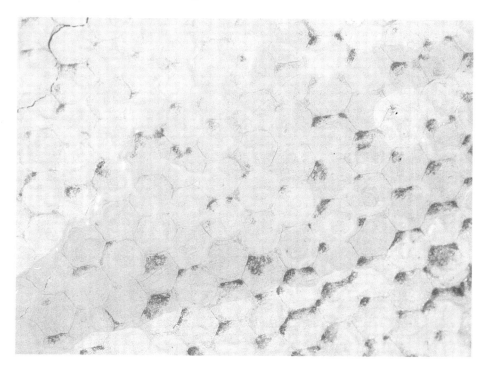

The Rourke Corporation, Inc.
Vero Beach, Florida 32964

PHOTO CREDITS:
All photos © Lynn M. Stone

ACKNOWLEDGMENT:
The author thanks the following for their support and assistance in the preparation of this book: May's Honey Farm, Harvard, IL; Harry Patterson

EDITORIAL SERVICES:
Susan Albury

CREATIVE SERVICES:
East Coast Studios, Merritt Island, FL

Library of Congress Cataloging-in-Publication Data

Stone, Lynn M.
  Honey farms / by Lynn M. Stone
    p. cm. — (Funky farms)
  Summary: Describes the physical characteristics and habits of honeybees and how they are raised on farms across the United States.
  ISBN 0-86593-540-8
  1. Bee culture Juvenile literature. 2. Honeybee Juvenile literature. [1. Bee culture. 2. Honeybee. 3. Bees.] I. Title. II. Series: Stone, Lynn M. Funky farms.
SF523.5.S76 1999
638'.1—dc21   99-25305
                                                                  CIP

Printed in the USA

CONTENTS

HONEYBEES

To see honeybees at their busy, buzzing best, visit an apple orchard in May, when the apple blossoms bloom.

Blossoms are tasty to honeybees because they hold **nectar** (NEK tur). They also hold **pollen** (PAH lun), which looks like yellow chalk dust. It helps plants **reproduce** (ree pruh DOOSS), or make more plants. But to do its job, pollen must be moved from one flower to another.

Honeybees move pollen as they fly from flower to flower. Some of the pollen that a honeybee picks up from one flower rubs off on the next. Without knowing it, the bees are **pollinating** (PAH luh nate ing) the flower.

Worker honeybees visit flowers to gather nectar and pollen. Nectar is the main raw ingredient in honey.

Nectar is a sweet liquid in the flower. Honeybees collect nectar and make honey from it. For the honeybee, both honey and pollen are food.

In some ways, honeybees are like most other insects. They have six legs, four wings, and a soft, boneless body. But in other ways, honeybees are amazing.

Honeybees can tell by smell if the other bees in their home, called a hive, belong there. If a bee from another hive tries to enter, guard bees attack and kill it.

Perhaps more amazing is the honeybee's "dance." By certain body movements back at the hive, scout honeybees can show other honeybees in what direction to fly to find flowers!

Honeybees swarm around a beekeeper. He's protected by heavy clothes, gloves, and a wire veil.

HONEY FARMS

To most people, honeybees are of interest because they make honey. Honey is a syruplike, golden liquid used on and in many foods. Honeybees are the only kind of bees that make more honey than they need.

Some honey farmers, or beekeepers, keep bees as a hobby. But others raise thousands of bees and make their living by selling honey and **beeswax** (BEEZ waks). All honey farms, large or small, are called **apiaries** (AY pee air eez).

A hive may hold 50,000-60,000 honeybees, but only the queen lays eggs. She may lay as many as 1,000 eggs daily.

BEEHIVES

Beekeepers in North America tend millions of hives. The beekeeper sets up the hives. The honeybees live in them.

Each hive looks like a group of white boxes, one atop or next to the other.

The hive holds a queen bee, tens of thousands of female **worker** (WUR kur) bees, and hundreds of male **drone** (DRONE) bees.

The queen lays eggs. The workers gather pollen and nectar. Drones tend the queen and eggs.

Honey farms produce honey and beeswax. The bee on the wax is not a honeybee but a yellow jacket. It was drawn by the sweet smell.

11

Waxy frames dripping with honey are sent through a machine called an extractor. Heat and motion help separate honey from wax.

At the end of the extraction process, honey pours into a stainless steel tank.

HOW HONEY FARMS BEGAN

Thousands of years ago, someone tasted honey from the hive of wild honeybees. The taste was a big hit!

Not long afterward, people learned to move **swarms** (SWARMZ) of honeybees. That meant that honeybees could be kept nearby. No one had to hunt in the forest for honey.

This beekeeper is using a smoker to help settle angry honeybees at the hive.

People made hives from hollow logs and baskets turned upside down.

Settlers who came to North America from Europe brought honeybees with them. By the late 1700s, honeybees were buzzing around much of the eastern United States.

This swarm of wild honeybees built its hive of honeycomb under a porch overhang.

WHERE HONEY FARMS ARE

Pioneers from the eastern United States brought honeybees into the American West. Today, honeybees are found throughout much of North America.

With honeybees widespread, honey farms are widespread as well, north, south, east, and west.

Honey farmers often put their hives near fields or orchards. The flowers of vegetable and fruit crops give the bees plenty of food. At the same time, the bees help crop farmers by pollinating their plants.

In the autumn apple season, these hives are quiet. Each spring, however, the orchard hums with the visits of honeybees to apple blossoms.

RAISING HONEYBEES

Beekeepers often buy their first swarm of bees. Sometimes they find a wild swarm and bring it to a hive. A beekeeper may have as many as 25 hives at one location.

Inside a basic hive are frames on which the bees build honeycomb. Honeycomb is made of beeswax. Bees store honey in the comb.

To gather honey, a beekeeper removes the frames with their honeycomb. A machine spins the honeycomb and separates the honey from the beeswax.

A beekeeper inspects a frame from his hive. The frames go to a honey farm's processing machines for the removal of honey.

Worker bees can sting, so a beekeeper dresses carefully. A veil, often made of wire, protects the beekeeper's face.

Honeybees don't like visitors coming to their hives, so beekeepers sometimes pump smoke around the hive they plan to open. Smoke settles honeybees down while the beekeeper tends to the hive.

Honeybees are busiest in June and July. As flowers disappear, honeybees are less active.

During winter, the bees remain in or close to their hives. There they live on the honey they stored up during the warm months.

GLOSSARY

apiary (AY pee air ee) — a honey farm; a place where bees are kept in hives by people

beeswax (BEEZ waks) — creamy colored wax that bees make in their bodies and use to build honeycomb, where honey and bees' eggs are stored in seperate cells (pockets)

drone (DRONE) — a male honeybee

nectar (NEK tur) — a sweet liquid made by plants and used by honeybees to make honey

pollen (PAH lun) — dustlike grains produced by seed-bearing plants and used when plants make new plants (reproduction)

pollinating (PAH luh nate ing) — the process of moving pollen from one plant to another

reproduce (ree pruh DOOSS) — to make more of the same plant or animal

swarm (SWARM) — a great number of honeybees with their queen; a colony of honeybees

worker (WUR kur) — a female honeybee that works to gather pollen and nectar

INDEX

FURTHER READING

Find out more about honey bees with these helpful books and information sites:
Pringle, Laurence. *Killer Bees.* New York: Morrow Junior Books, 1990
Rowan, James. *Honeybees.* Vero Beach, FL: Rourke, 1993

American Beekeeping Federation   P.O Box 1038   Jesup, GA 31545   www.abfnet.org
National Honey Board   421 21st Avenue, Ste. 203   Longmont, CO 80501-1421   www.honey.com